CROSS STITCH

WELCOME BABY

DURENE JONES

Tuva Publishing

www.tuvapublishing.com

Address Merkez Mah. Cavusbasi Cad. No:71
Cekmekoy - Istanbul 34782 / Turkey
Tel: +9 0216 642 62 62

Cross Stitch Welcome Baby

First Print 2017 / December

All Global Copyrights Belong To
Tuva Tekstil ve Yayıncılık Ltd.

Content Cross Stitch

Editor in Chief Ayhan DEMİRPEHLİVAN
Project Editor Kader DEMİRPEHLİVAN
Designer Durene JONES
Technical Editors Leyla ARAS, Büşra ESER
Graphic Designers Ömer ALP, Abdullah BAYRAKÇI, Zilal ÖNEL
Photograph Tuva Publishing

ISBN 978-605-9192-31-6

Printing House
Bilnet Matbaacılık ve Yayıncılık A.Ş.

 TuvaYayincilik TuvaPublishing
 TuvaYayincilik TuvaPublishing

CONTENTS

INTRODUCTION

In this my latest book of cross stitch designs I'm overjoyed to introduce to you designs to celebrate the arrival of a new baby in the family. And I've included lots of ideas to celebrate this special time, with a collection of designs suitable for girls and boys from birth through to toddler and onto young child, so you can choose the ideal pattern for your little ones, or sew something as a gift to present to a friend.

A lot of the designs in the book are smaller in size, and would be ideal for use on cards, tags, gifts, decorating clothing and other home crafting projects, or because of their overall look, the smaller designs could be combined easily to create larger sampler style designs. However some of the patterns are a little larger, so if you want a more challenging stitch, something that would take you a little longer to sew, then you can also find them in this book. Which makes this a great book for all stitching levels and abilities.

I've really enjoyed designing the charts for this book to help you commemorate this happy time, and I hope you will get just as much enjoyment from stitching them.

Happy Stitching!

Durene Jones

PROJECT GALLERY

PAGE 14

PAGE 14

PAGE 15

PAGE 18

PAGE 19

PAGE 15

PAGE 19

PAGE 21

PAGE 21

PAGE 23

PAGE 25

PAGE 25

PAGE 25

PAGE 23

PAGE 27

PAGE 29

PAGE 29

PAGE 33

PAGE 35

PAGE 37

Julie Worthing
12 • 3 • 18   7lb 8oz

PAGE 31   PAGE 33   PAGE 35

PAGE 37

PAGE 39

PAGE 43   PAGE 47

PAGE 42   PAGE 43   PAGE 47   PAGE 46

PAGE 49   PAGE 52   PAGE 53

PAGE 55

PAGE 57

PAGE 63

PAGE 63

PAGE 61

PAGE 66

PAGE 67

PAGE 59

PAGE 70

PAGE 71

PAGE 73

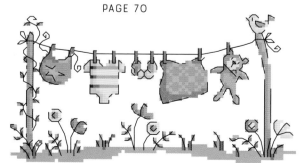

PAGE 75

PAGE 78

PAGE 78

PAGE 85

PAGE 79

PAGE 87

PAGE 85

PAGE 82

PAGE 87

PAGE 89

PAGE 89

PAGE 83

James
Simpson

24.8.17
7lb 6oz

PAGE 92

Rebecca
Simpson

24.8.17
7lb 6oz

PAGE 94

Rebecca
Simpson

24.8.17

7lb 6oz

Your New Arrival

The arrival of a new baby to the family is always a beautiful event. A hand stitched gift or card especially made for the new baby is a treasure to make and recieve and makes a special keepsake for generations to come.

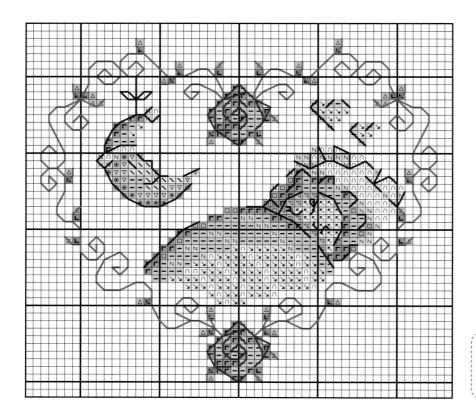

DMC
Mouliné
Stranded Cotton Art. 117

☐☐	415	▽▽	744
N N	762	＼＼	745
∩∩	B5200	▽	945
L L	166	✕✕	3770
▵▵	165		Backstitch
┌┌	603	╱	3799
‐‐	605	╱	581
＼	818	╱	3831
◉◉	743		

Fabric DMC 28 ct Linen Fabric
(DM 432 SO/B5200) • **Colour** White
Needle DMC Cross-Stitch No:26 (Art:1771/3)
Cross Stitch 2 strands • **Backstitch** 1 strand

DMC
Mouliné
Stranded Cotton Art. 117

☐☐	415	✕✕	818
N N	762	▽	945
∩∩	B5200	✕✕	3770
T T	913		Backstitch
◣◣	955	╱	3799
◉◉	434	╱	3831
★★	436	╱	3818
⫠⫠	437		French Knot
✕✕	738	◉	603
┌┌	603		
‐‐	605		

Fabric DMC 28 ct Linen Fabric
(DM 432 SO/B5200) • **Colour** White
Needle DMC Cross-Stitch No:26 (Art:1771/3)
Cross Stitch 2 strands • **Backstitch** 1 strand
French Knot 2 strands

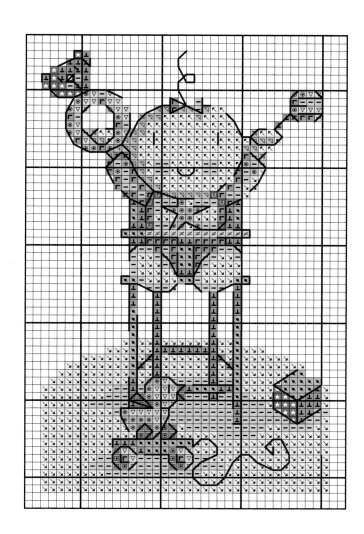

Mouliné
Stranded Cotton Art. 117

▦	434	◉◉	743	
★★	436	▽▽	744	
⊥⊥	437	◥◥	945	
⋰⋰	738	⋰⋰	3770	
≠≠	739		Backstitch	
UU	602	╱	3779	
┌┌	603			
==	605			
⋰⋰	818			
▣▣	3854			

┌─────────────────────────────────┐
Fabric DMC 28 ct Linen Fabric
(DM 432 SO/B5200) • **Colour** White
Needle DMC Cross-Stitch No:26 (Art:1771/3)
Cross Stitch 2 strands • **Backstitch** 1 strand
└─────────────────────────────────┘

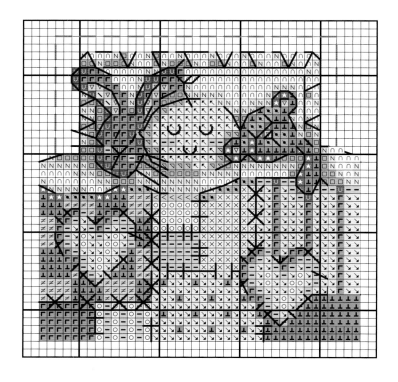

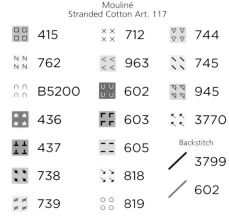

Mouliné
Stranded Cotton Art. 117

□□	415	××	712	▽▽	744	
NN	762	<<	963	⋰⋰	745	
∩∩	B5200	UU	602	◥◥	945	
★★	436	┌┌	603	⋰⋰	3770	
⊥⊥	437	==	605		Backstitch	
⋰⋰	738	⋰⋰	818	╱	3799	
≠≠	739	○○	819	╱	602	

┌─────────────────────────────────┐
Fabric DMC 28 ct Linen Fabric
(DM 432 SO/B5200) • **Colour** White
Needle DMC Cross-Stitch No:26 (Art:1771/3)
Cross Stitch 2 strands • **Backstitch** 1 strand
└─────────────────────────────────┘

A Bundle of Joy

What could be nicer for a new mother and her baby than to recieve a hand-made gift featuring her new bundle of joy? Why not use these designs to stitch a card to congratulate a new family.

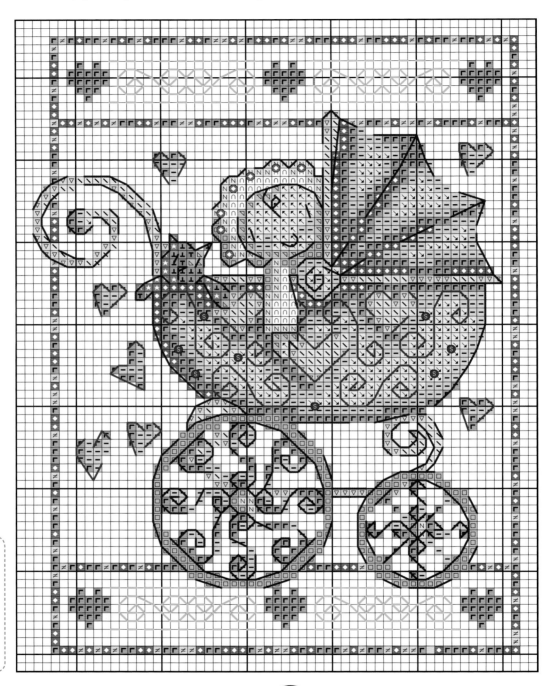

Fabric DMC 28 ct Linen
Fabric
(DM 432 SO/B5200) •
Colour White
Needle DMC Cross-Stitch
No:26 (Art:1771/3)
Cross Stitch 2 strands •
Backstitch 1 strand
French Knot 2 strands

DMC
Mouliné
Stranded Cotton Art. 117

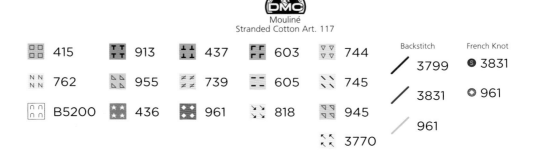

415	913	437	603	744
762	955	739	605	745
B5200	436	961	818	945
				3770

Backstitch
3799
3831
961

French Knot
3831
961

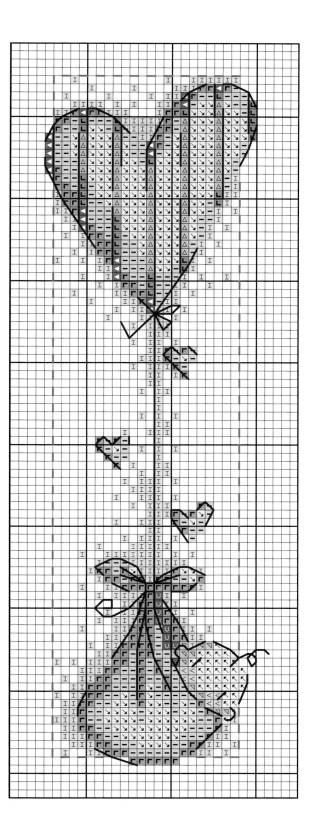

Mouliné
Stranded Cotton Art. 117

◀◀	581	⋰⋰	818
LL	166	⊻⊻	945
△△	165	⊼⊼	3770
<<	963	II I	747
U·U U·U	602	**Backstitch**	
┌┌ ┌┌	603	╱	3799
‐‐ ‐‐	605	╱	961

Fabric DMC 28 ct Linen Fabric
(DM 432 SO/B5200) • **Colour** White
Needle DMC Cross-Stitch No:26 (Art:1771/3)
Cross Stitch 2 strands • **Backstitch** 1 strand

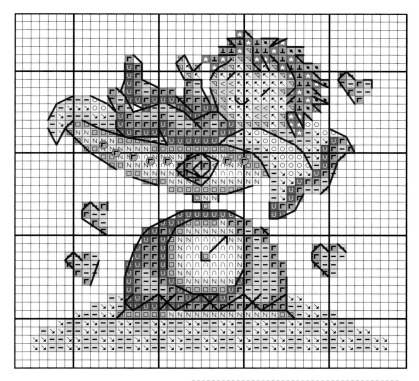

Fabric DMC 28 ct Linen Fabric
(DM 432 SO/B5200) • **Colour** White
Needle DMC Cross-Stitch No:26 (Art:1771/3)
Cross Stitch 2 strands • **Backstitch** 1 strand
French Knot 2 strands

Mouliné
Stranded Cotton Art. 117

🔲 415	★★ 436	<< 963	‐‐ 605	⊻⊻ 945	**Backstitch**
N N 762	⊥⊥ 437	U·U 602	⋰⋰ 818	⊼⊼ 3770	╱ 3799
⌒⌒ B5200	⋰⋰ 738	┌┌ 603	○○ 819		**French Knot** ● 603

Blanket Time

It's easy to transform plain cot linen into something unique for a special baby. Why not use these motifs, with their soothing greens and neutral browns they are ideal for a restful sleep and would suit both boys and girls.

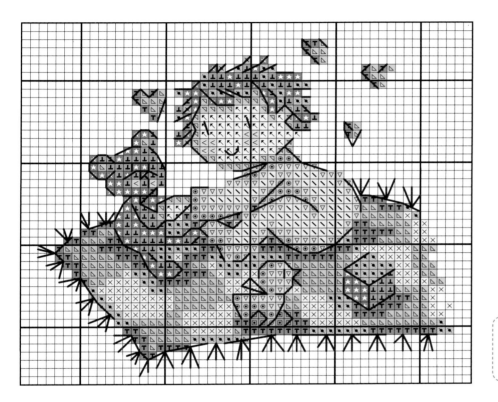

Mouliné
Stranded Cotton Art. 117

TT	913	3854	
955		743	
436		744	
437		745	
738		945	
712		3770	
963		Backstitch 3799	

Fabric DMC 28 ct Linen Fabric
(DM 432 SO/B5200) • **Colour** White
Needle DMC Cross-Stitch No:26 (Art:1771/3)
Cross Stitch 2 strands • **Backstitch** 1 strand

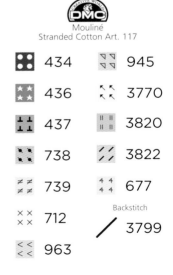

Mouliné
Stranded Cotton Art. 117

434		945	
436		3770	
437		3820	
738		3822	
739		677	
712		Backstitch 3799	
963			

Fabric DMC 28 ct Linen Fabric
(DM 432 SO/B5200) • **Colour** White
Needle DMC Cross-Stitch No:26 (Art:1771/3)
Cross Stitch 2 strands • **Backstitch** 1 strand

Babies Wardrobe

Preparing the first set of clothes for your new arrival is an important event. Why not use some of the bright and colourful motifs in this book to decorate some of your little ones new wardrobe.

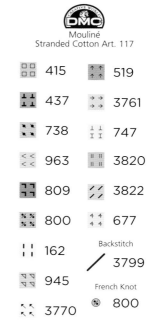

Mouliné
Stranded Cotton Art. 117

415		519	
437		3761	
738		747	
963		3820	
809		3822	
800		677	
162		**Backstitch** 3799	
945		**French Knot** 800	
3770			

Fabric DMC 28 ct Linen Fabric
(DM 432 SO/B5200) • **Colour** White
Needle DMC Cross-Stitch No:26 (Art:1771/3)
Cross Stitch 2 strands • **Backstitch** 1 strand
French Knot 2 strands

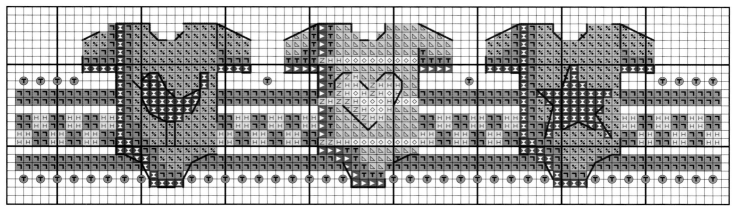

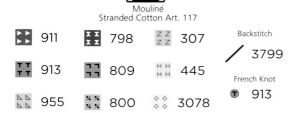

Mouliné
Stranded Cotton Art. 117

911	798	307
913	809	445
955	800	3078

Backstitch 3799

French Knot 913

Fabric DMC 28 ct Linen Fabric
(DM 432 SO/B5200) • **Colour** White
Needle DMC Cross-Stitch No:26 (Art:1771/3)
Cross Stitch 2 strands • **Backstitch** 1 strand
French Knot 2 strands

Mini Pictures Trio

Small designs are ideal to be sewn as quick and easy pictures to decorate the nursery.
Sew them all in blues, or all in pinks, to suit your needs. Or alternatively sew them all
and arrange them as a nursery hanging ornament or mobile.

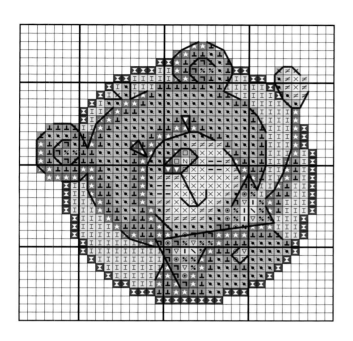

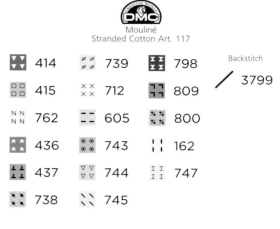

Mouliné
Stranded Cotton Art. 117

414		739		798	**Backstitch**	
415		712		809	/	3799
762		605		800		
436		743		162		
437		744		747		
738		745				

Fabric DMC 28 ct Linen Fabric
(DM 432 SO/B5200) • **Colour** White
Needle DMC Cross-Stitch No:26 (Art:1771/3)
Cross Stitch 2 strands • **Backstitch** 1 strand

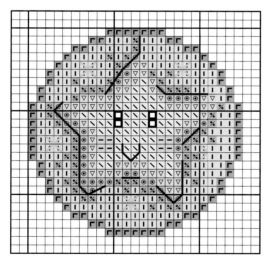

Mouliné
Stranded Cotton Art. 117

3799		743		800	**Backstitch**	
603		744		162	/	3799
605		745			/	743

Fabric DMC 28 ct Linen Fabric
(DM 432 SO/B5200) • **Colour** White
Needle DMC Cross-Stitch No:26 (Art:1771/3)
Cross Stitch 2 strands • **Backstitch** 1 strand

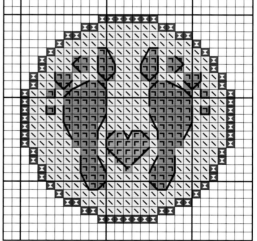

Mouliné
Stranded Cotton Art. 117

603		809	
745		**Backstitch**	
798		/	3799

Fabric DMC 28 ct Linen Fabric
(DM 432 SO/B5200) • **Colour** White
Needle DMC Cross-Stitch No:26 (Art:1771/3)
Cross Stitch 2 strands • **Backstitch** 1 strand

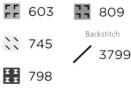

Sail Away

This charming design of little blue boats and yachts would make an ideal picture for any little boys nursery. You could add a name and even a weight and date of birth under the boats to make it into an adorable birth sampler. And why not add buttons for the round windows on the boats and use felt for the flags and buntings to add a lovely handmade feel.

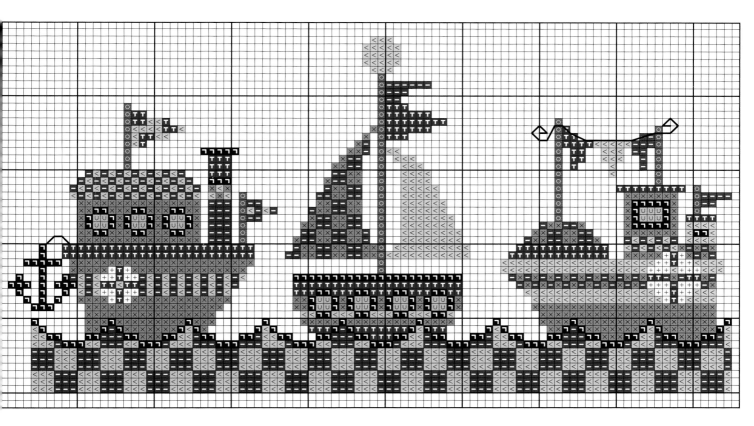

Mouliné
Stranded Cotton Art. 117

U U / U U	415	o o / o o	435	x x / x x	809	Backstitch
+ + / + +	B5200	■	796	< < / < <	3761	/ 310
T T / T T	817	▬	798			

Fabric DMC 28 ct Linen Fabric
(DM 432 SO/B5200) • **Colour** White
Needle DMC Cross-Stitch No:26 (Art:1771/3)
Cross Stitch 2 strands • **Backstitch** 1 strand

Hearts and Flowers

Two lovely little sweet designs which are sure to delight any baby or toddler and bring joy to the nursery. They are themed for you to combine them in any number of ways, the possibilities are endless. Why not use the bird and heart as the central motif for a cushion, with the flowers repeated on an Aida band with matching edging and sewn at the top and bottom of the cushion.

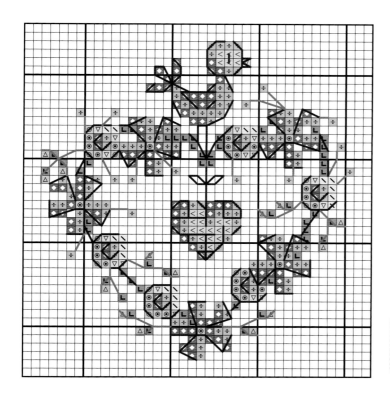

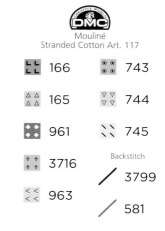

DMC
Mouliné
Stranded Cotton Art. 117

L L / L L	166	⊙⊙ / ⊙⊙	743
△△ / △△	165	▽▽ / ▽▽	744
◈◈ / ◈◈	961	╲╲	745
∴∴ / ∴∴	3716		**Backstitch**
<< / <<	963	/	3799
		/	581

Fabric DMC 28 ct Linen Fabric
(DM 432 SO/B5200) • **Colour** White
Needle DMC Cross-Stitch No:26 (Art:1771/3)
Cross Stitch 2 strands • **Backstitch** 1 strand

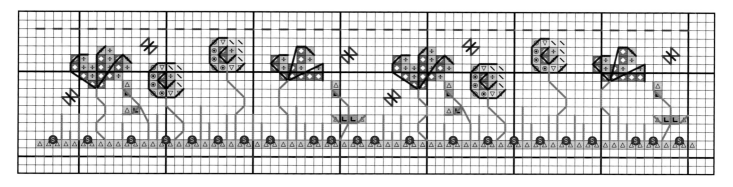

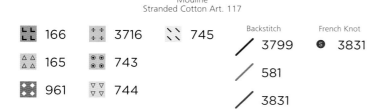

DMC
Mouliné
Stranded Cotton Art. 117

L L / L L	166	∴∴ / ∴∴	3716	╲╲	745	
△△ / △△	165	⊙⊙ / ⊙⊙	743			
◈◈ / ◈◈	961	▽▽ / ▽▽	744			

Backstitch
/ 3799
/ 581
/ 3831

French Knot
Ⓢ 3831

Fabric DMC 28 ct Linen Fabric
(DM 432 SO/B5200) • **Colour** White
Needle DMC Cross-Stitch No:26 (Art:1771/3)
Cross Stitch 2 strands • **Backstitch** 1 strand
French Knot 2 strands

Little Birds Birth Sampler

The simplicity of this birth sampler makes it a joy to stitch. It would look lovely framed on a nursery wall, or stitched as the front of a baby journal. The design can easily be personalised using the alphabet provided.

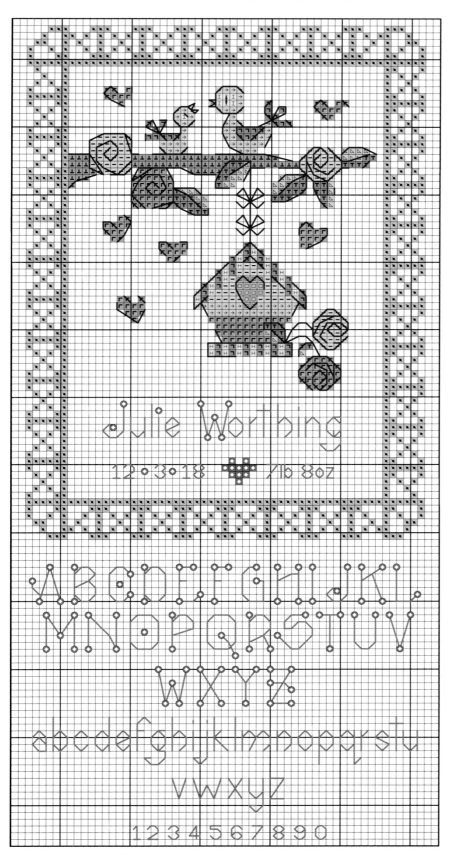

DMC

Mouliné
Stranded Cotton Art. 117

⊡⊡	415
TT	913
◣◣	955
⊥⊥	437
∴∴	738
✕✕	961
⊏⊏	603
∶∶	605
⅃⅃	809
H H	445
→→	3761
I I	747

Backstitch

╱	3799
╱	961

French Knot

◉	961

Fabric DMC 28 ct Linen Fabric
(DM 432 SO/B5200) • **Colour** White
Needle DMC Cross-Stitch No:26 (Art:1771/3)
Cross Stitch 2 strands • **Backstitch** 1 strand
French Knot 2 strands

It's The Little Things

Often when preparing for a new arrival it's the little things that can be forgotten. But a small hand stitched gift can be just as precious and treasured as any other, and it shows the new family just how special they are. The small motifs in this book are ideal to sew on bags, bootees, bibs, cot blankets, even curtain trims or to make hanging mobiles. I'm sure you will see more and more possibilities once you get started stitcing for baby.

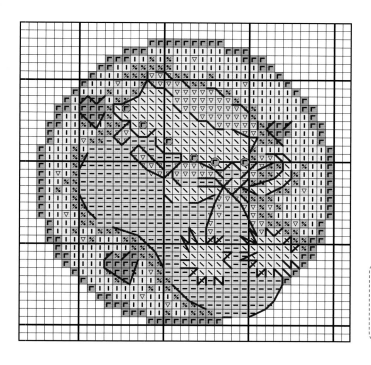

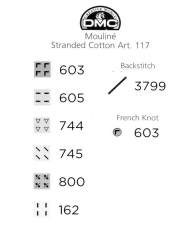

Mouliné
Stranded Cotton Art. 117

603		Backstitch
605		/ 3799
744		
745		French Knot
800		⊙ 603
162		

Fabric DMC 28 ct Linen Fabric
(DM 432 SO/B5200) • **Colour** White
Needle DMC Cross-Stitch No:26 (Art:1771/3)
Cross Stitch 2 strands • **Backstitch** 1 strand
French Knot 2 strands

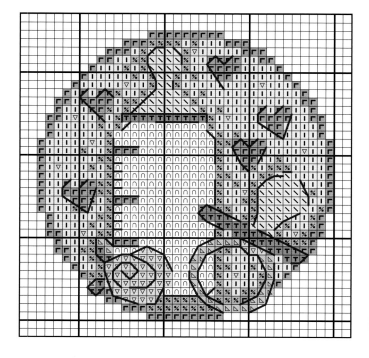

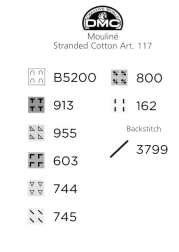

Mouliné
Stranded Cotton Art. 117

B5200		800	
913		162	
955			Backstitch
603			/ 3799
744			
745			

Fabric DMC 28 ct Linen Fabric
(DM 432 SO/B5200) • **Colour** White
Needle DMC Cross-Stitch No:26 (Art:1771/3)
Cross Stitch 2 strands • **Backstitch** 1 strand

THURSDAY

TUESDAY

WEDNESDAY

34

Butterflies Flutter By

Two very different, but equally charming designs of butterflies, but both with happy smiling faces, beautiful patterns on their wings, and sewn using bright fresh colours. They are also of a size that would make them suitable for any number of things. Why not use the butterfly in a heart to decorate the bib of a little girl's dress, or stitch the butterfly in a circle as an embellishment for a greeting card.

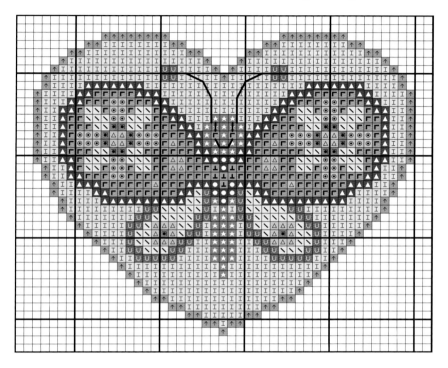

Mouliné
Stranded Cotton Art. 117

△△	166	＼＼	745
●●	434	▲▲	208
★★	436	▪▪	209
⊥⊥	437	↑↑	519
U·U	602	I I	747
ГГ	603		Backstitch
⊙⊙	743	╱	310

Fabric DMC 28 ct Linen Fabric
(DM 432 SO/B5200) • *Colour* White
Needle DMC Cross-Stitch No:26 (Art:1771/3)
Cross Stitch 2 strands • *Backstitch* 1 strand

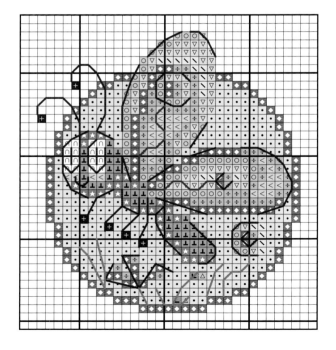

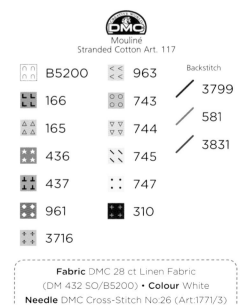

Mouliné
Stranded Cotton Art. 117

∩∩	B5200	＜＜	963		Backstitch
ԼԼ	166	○○	743	╱	3799
△△	165	▽▽	744	╱	581
★★	436	＼＼	745	╱	3831
⊥⊥	437	∷	747		
✕✕	961	✛✛	310		
÷÷	3716				

Fabric DMC 28 ct Linen Fabric
(DM 432 SO/B5200) • *Colour* White
Needle DMC Cross-Stitch No:26 (Art:1771/3)
Cross Stitch 2 strands • *Backstitch* 1 strand

Animal Hearts

These bright and colourful animal designs with their sweet patchwork hearts and little roses in the corners would make ideal greeting cards or small pictures. Or why not sew only the heart sections and stitch together on ribbon to make an adorable hanging or fun bunting.

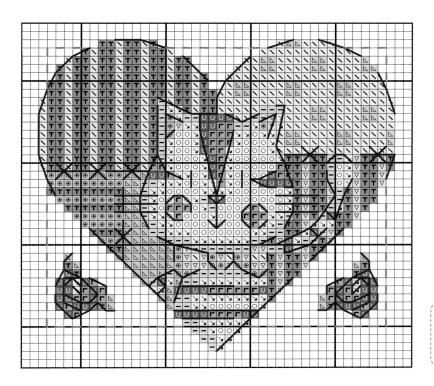

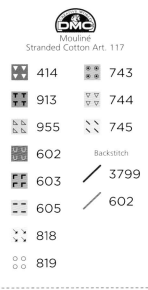

Mouliné
Stranded Cotton Art. 117

414		743		
913		744		
955		745		
602		Backstitch		
603		3799		
605		602		
818				
819				

Fabric DMC 28 ct Linen Fabric
(DM 432 SO/B5200) • **Colour** White
Needle DMC Cross-Stitch No:26 (Art:1771/3)
Cross Stitch 2 strands • **Backstitch** 1 strand

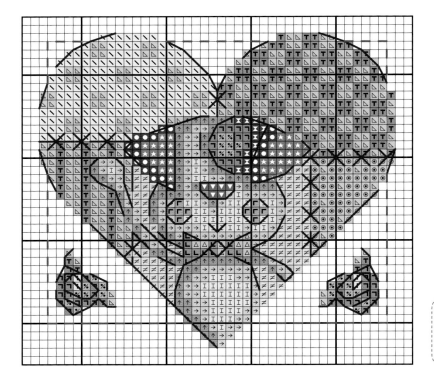

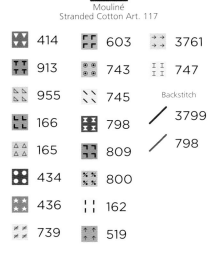

Mouliné
Stranded Cotton Art. 117

414		603		3761	
913		743		747	
955		745		Backstitch	
166		798		3799	
165		809		798	
434		800			
436		162			
739		519			

Fabric DMC 28 ct Linen Fabric
(DM 432 SO/B5200) • **Colour** White
Needle DMC Cross-Stitch No:26 (Art:1771/3)
Cross Stitch 2 strands • **Backstitch** 1 strand

All in a Row

Cute baby bibs in sweet pinks and greens, adorned with teddies, hearts and little cats would make a lovely addition to any nursery. Use them as a repeat pattern to decorate home furnishings or bedding. And why not replace the hearts with little heart shaped buttons or cut out felt for a more hand crafted feel.

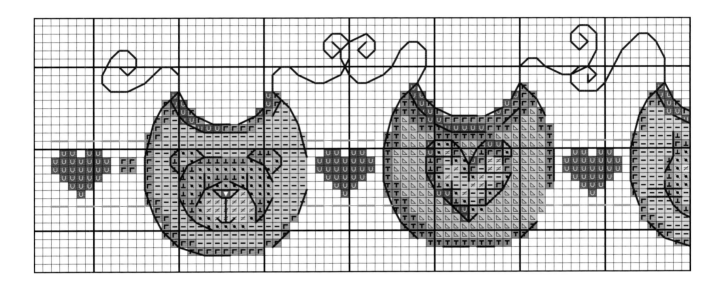

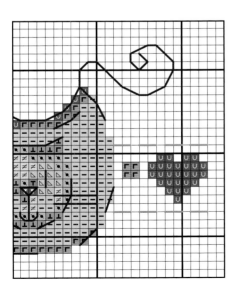

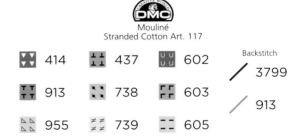

DMC
Mouliné
Stranded Cotton Art. 117

414	437	602
913	738	603
955	739	605

Backstitch

3799

913

Fabric DMC 28 ct Linen Fabric
(DM 432 SO/B5200) • **Colour** White
Needle DMC Cross-Stitch No:26 (Art:1771/3)
Cross Stitch 2 strands • **Backstitch** 1 strand

A Busy Boy's Day

Flying a kite in the sunshine, playing with building blocks or taking your teddy on a picnic, all the activities that keep a busy boy happy. These designs with their quite blues and fresh greens are evocative of long summer days, of playing outside without a care in the world.

Mouliné
Stranded Cotton Art. 117

415	**Backstitch**
762	/ 3799
B5200	/ 581
166	/ 798
165	**French Knot**
434	O 3799
436	⊙ 800
437	
963	
743	
744	
745	
809	
800	
162	
945	
3770	
747	
3820	
3822	

Fabric DMC 28 ct Linen Fabric
(DM 432 SO/B5200) • **Colour** White
Needle DMC Cross-Stitch No:26 (Art:1771/3)
Cross Stitch 2 strands • **Backstitch** 1 strand
French Knot 2 strands

Mouliné
Stranded Cotton Art. 117

				Backstitch
415		745		/ 3799
762		809		/ 581
B5200		800		/ 798
166		162		
165		945		
436		3770		
437		747		
963		3820		
743		3822		
744				

Fabric DMC 28 ct Linen Fabric
(DM 432 SO/B5200) • **Colour** White
Needle DMC Cross-Stitch No:26 (Art:1771/3)
Cross Stitch 2 strands • **Backstitch** 1 strand

Mouliné
Stranded Cotton Art. 117

				Backstitch
415		743		/ 3799
762		744		/ 581
B5200		745		/ 798
166		945		
165		3770		
436		747		
437		3820		
738		3822		
963				

Fabric DMC 28 ct Linen Fabric
(DM 432 SO/B5200) • **Colour** White
Needle DMC Cross-Stitch No:26 (Art:1771/3)
Cross Stitch 2 strands • **Backstitch** 1 strand

A Busy Girl's Day

Playing with balloons, chatting to butterflies, and collecting posies are all the activities that keep a busy girl happy. These designs with their sweet pinks and fresh greens are evocative of hot, endless summers, of playing outside without a care in the world.

DMC
Mouliné
Stranded Cotton Art. 117

Symbol	Colour		
N N N N	762	**Backstitch**	
∩ ∩ ∩ ∩	B5200	╱	3799
L L L L	166	╱	581
△ △ △ △	165	╱	3831
434			
★★ ★★	436	**French Knot**	
⊥⊥ ⊥⊥	437	●	3831
961			
✛✛ ✛✛	3716	⋂	B5200
< < < <	963		
° ° ° °	819		
⊙ ⊙ ⊙ ⊙	743		
▽ ▽ ▽ ▽	744		
＼ ＼ ＼ ＼	745		
▽ ▽ ▽ ▽	945		
⌐ ⌐ ⌐ ⌐	3770		
I I I I	747		

Fabric DMC 28 ct Linen Fabric
(DM 432 SO/B5200) • **Colour** White
Needle DMC Cross-Stitch No:26 (Art:1771/3)
Cross Stitch 2 strands • **Backstitch** 1 strand
French Knot 2 strands

Mouliné
Stranded Cotton Art. 117

N N N	762	○ ○	819
∩ ∩	B5200	⊙ ⊙	743
L L L L	166	▽ ▽	744
△ △	165	＼ ＼	745
434		▽ ▽	945
★ ★	436	＾ ＾	3770
⊥ ⊥	437	I I I I	747
961			
÷ ÷	3716		
＜ ＜	963		

French Knot

○ 3799
Ⓢ 3831
ⓝ B5200

Backstitch
╱ 3799
╱ 581
╱ 3831

Fabric DMC 28 ct Linen Fabric
(DM 432 SO/B5200) • Colour White
Needle DMC Cross-Stitch No:26 (Art:1771/3)
Cross Stitch 2 strands • Backstitch 1 strand
French Knot 2 strands

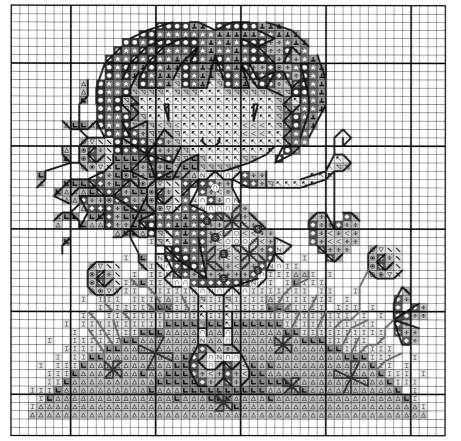

Mouliné
Stranded Cotton Art. 117

N N N	762	⊙ ⊙	743
∩ ∩	B5200	▽ ▽	744
L L L L	166	＼ ＼	745
△ △	165	▽ ▽	945
434		＾ ＾	3770
★ ★	436	I I I I	747
⊥ ⊥	437		
961			
÷ ÷	3716		
＜ ＜	963		

French Knot

Ⓢ 3831
ⓝ B5200

Backstitch
╱ 3799
╱ 581
╱ 3831

Fabric DMC 28 ct Linen Fabric
(DM 432 SO/B5200) • Colour White
Needle DMC Cross-Stitch No:26 (Art:1771/3)
Cross Stitch 2 strands • Backstitch 1 strand
French Knot 2 strands

Playtime Fun

Who wouldn't enjoy snuggling into a cuddly teddy, or riding on a friendly elephant? Decorate the nursery to create a lovely wonderous, fairytale environment using some of the larger designs in this book.

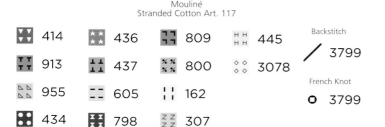

Mouliné
Stranded Cotton Art. 117

414	436	809	H H H 445
913	437	800	3078
955	605	162	
434	798	Z Z Z 307	

Backstitch
/ 3799

French Knot
O 3799

Fabric DMC 28 ct Linen Fabric
(DM 432 SO/B5200) • **Colour** White
Needle DMC Cross-Stitch No:26 (Art:1771/3)
Cross Stitch 2 strands • **Backstitch** 1 strand
French Knot 2 strands

Teddy Bear Cuddles

These adorable bears, a favourite of so many children would add a very special touch to any nursery, the blues are easily changed to suit your needs and would look equally lovely in either pinks or greens. Why not use this design to decorate a cot quilt and make a unique gift for the new arrival.

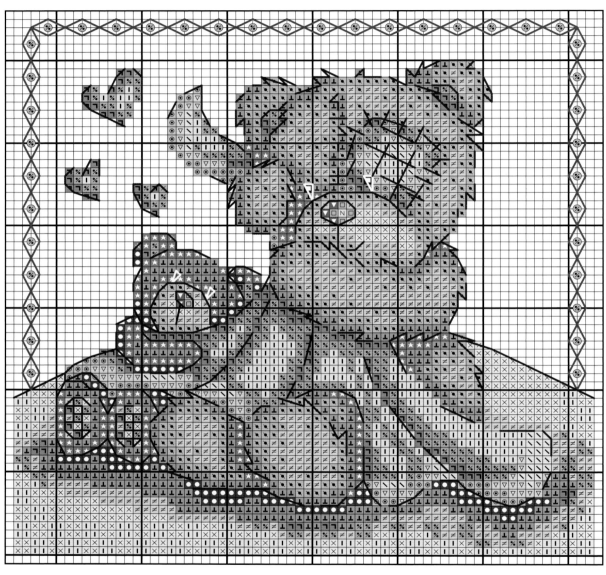

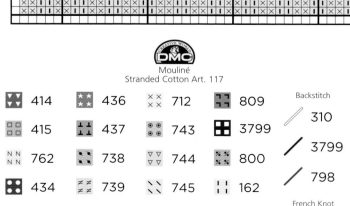

DMC
Mouliné
Stranded Cotton Art. 117

414	436	712	809	**Backstitch**
415	437	743	3799	310
762	738	744	800	3799
434	739	745	162	798

French Knot
800

Fabric DMC 28 ct Linen Fabric
(DM 432 SO/B5200) • **Colour** White
Needle DMC Cross-Stitch No:26 (Art:1771/3)
Cross Stitch 2 strands • **Backstitch** 1 strand
French Knot 2 strands

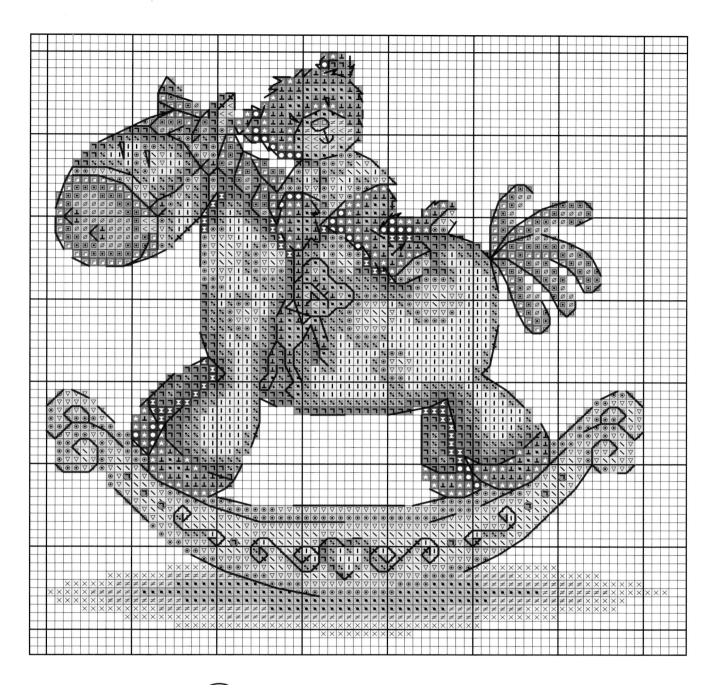

Mouliné
Stranded Cotton Art. 117

415	738	3853	▽▽ 744	800
434	739	3854	\\ 745	162
436	×× 712	∅∅ 3855	798	
437	<< 963	743	809	

Backstitch

/ 3799

French Knot

● 809

Fabric DMC 28 ct Linen Fabric
(DM 432 SO/B5200) • **Colour** White
Needle DMC Cross-Stitch No:26 (Art:1771/3)
Cross Stitch 2 strands • **Backstitch** 1 strand
French Knot 2 strands

Surprise!

The anticipation of a Jack-in-the-box opening can be a worrying thing, especially for a young child. But when he's this cute and happy looking it's like the return of an old friend, and fills you with nothing but excitement. This design would be great bordered with matching fabric and made into a cushion for you and baby to enjoy in the nursery.

Mouliné
Stranded Cotton Art. 117

L L / L L	166	739	745	945
165	603	209	3770
434	743	210	Backstitch
738	744	211	/ 3799

Fabric DMC 28 ct Linen Fabric (DM 432 SO/B5200) • **Colour** White
Needle DMC Cross-Stitch No:26 (Art:1771/3)
Cross Stitch 2 strands • **Backstitch** 1 strand

Teddy Bear Alphabet

Create all manner of exciting designs using this teddy bear alphabet. Sew the whole alphabet as wall decoration for a bedroom, nursery or playroom and use it as an early learning aid, sew a roomname plaque for a child, personalise clothing, or just sew a single initial as a card or ornament.

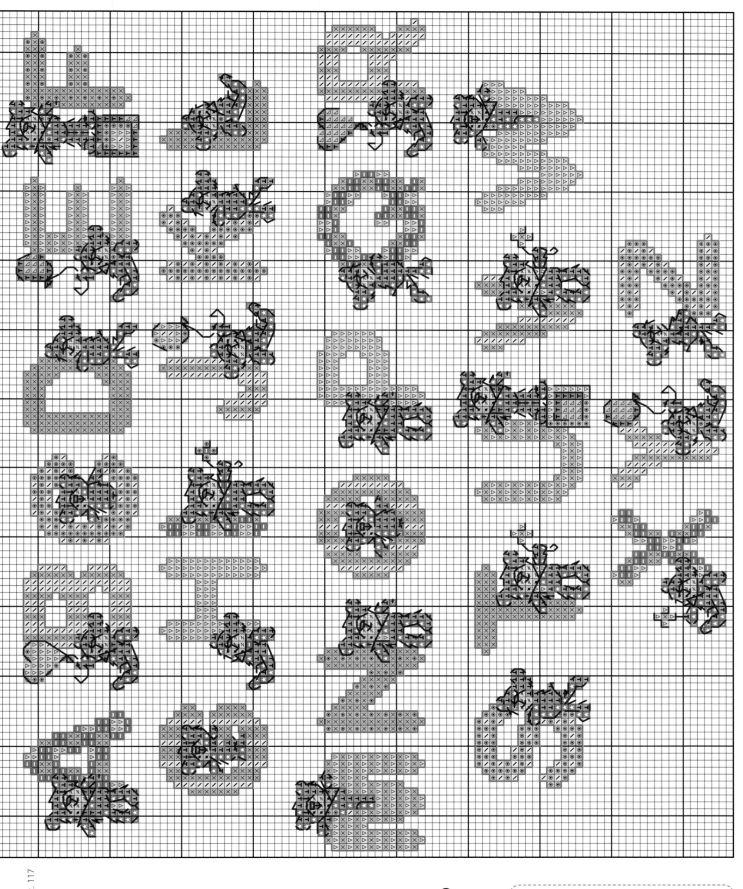

 DMC
Mouliné
Stranded Cotton Art. 117

912	913	954	955	436	437	738	739	743	744	745	Backstitch	3799	414

Fabric DMC 28 ct Linen Fabric
(DM 432 SO/B5200) • **Colour** White
Needle DMC Cross-Stitch No:26 (Art:1771/3)
Cross Stitch 2 strands • **Backstitch** 1 strand

Baby Birds & Butterflies

Baby birds, butterflies, little ladybirds and the promise of warm carefree days. All you need for a relaxing addition to a child's bedroom or nursery. Sew the whole alphabet as wall decoration for a bedroom, nursery or playroom and use it as an early learning aid, sew a room name plaque for a child, personalise clothing, or just sew a single initial as a card or ornament.

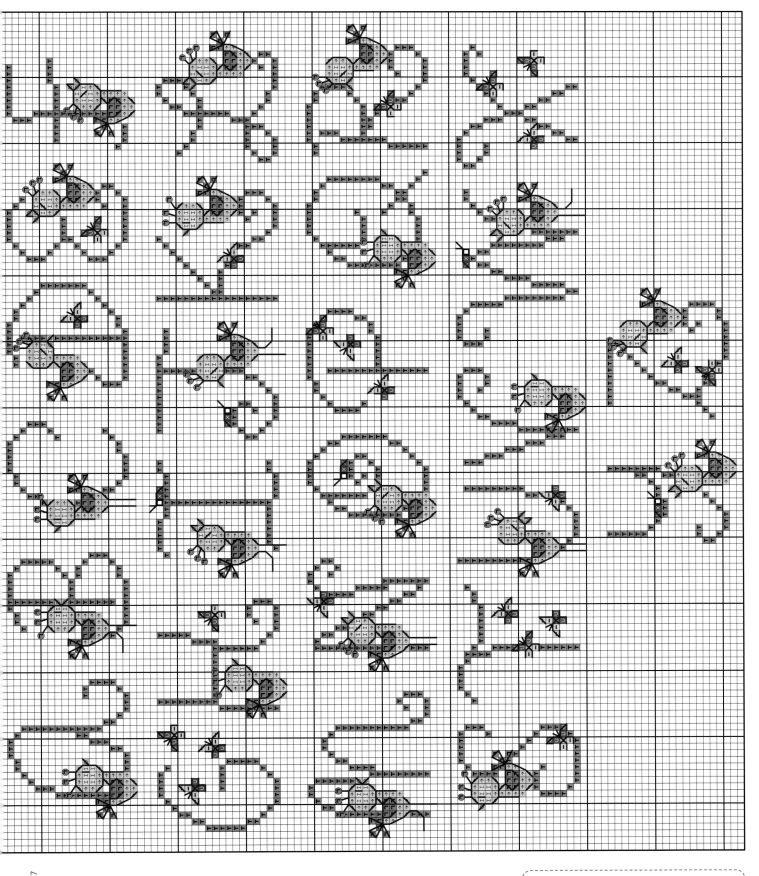

DMC Mouliné Stranded Cotton Art. 117

Symbol	Colour
⊞	3799
⊢⊢	913
✕✕	350
⊔⊔	602
⎮⎮	605
⊙⊙	743
⌐⌐	809
↑↑	3761
⊨⊨	747

Backstitch
╱ 3799

French Knot
● 809

Fabric DMC 28 ct Linen Fabric
(DM 432 SO/B5200) • **Colour** White
Needle DMC Cross-Stitch No:26 (Art:1771/3)
Cross Stitch 2 strands • **Backstitch** 1 strand
French Knot 2 strands

Soothing Sleep

Mobiles hung above babies cot soothe and aid sleep, with their gently twirling baby toys, and objects. Why not sew this cross stitched mobile complete with teddy, baby bootie, sleepy moon, roses and hearts and frame it to adorn the nursery wall, giving lots more for you and baby to see.

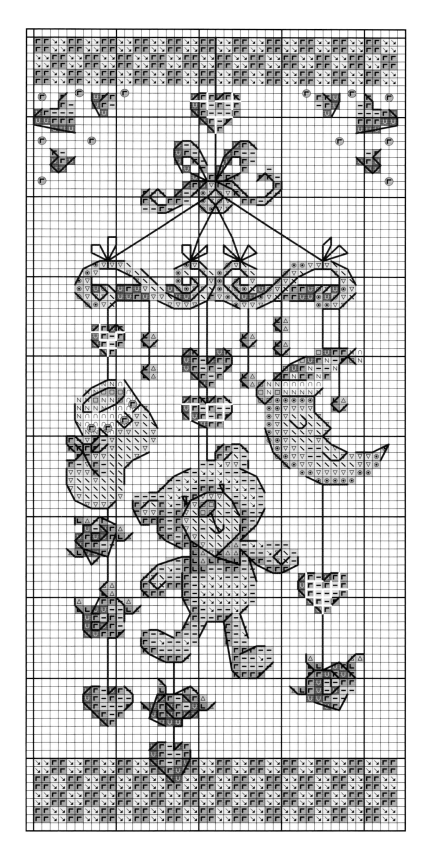

Mouliné
Stranded Cotton Art. 117

415	
762	
B5200	
166	
165	
602	
603	
605	
818	
743	
744	
745	

Backstitch

3799	
B5200	

French Knot

603	

Fabric DMC 28 ct Linen Fabric
(DM 432 SO/B5200) • Colour White
Needle DMC Cross-Stitch No:26 (Art:1771/3)
Cross Stitch 2 strands • Backstitch 1 strand
French Knot 2 strands

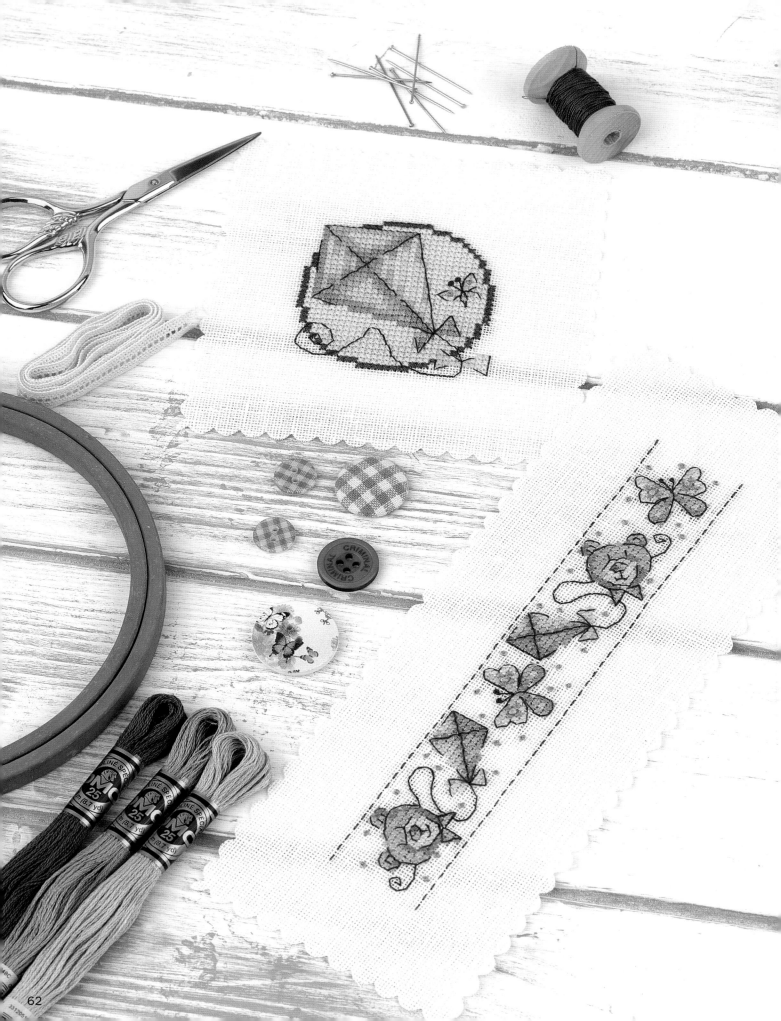

Adventure Awaits

Teddies, butterflies, birds and all manner of friendly animals await to accompany you on carefree adventures in these designs. Stitch them as wall art or as decoration for a nursery, and make up endless stories about the fun times you and your little one will have together.

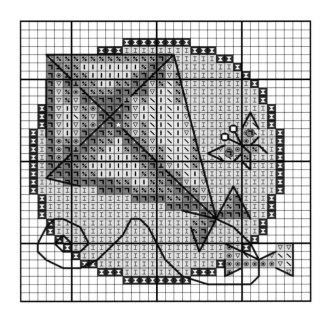

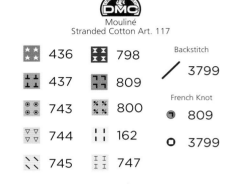

Mouliné
Stranded Cotton Art. 117

★★	436	✕✕	798	**Backstitch**
⊥⊥	437		809	╱ 3799
⊙⊙	743	✕✕	800	**French Knot**
▽▽	744	‖	162	◐ 809
╲╲	745	II	747	O 3799

Fabric DMC 28 ct Linen Fabric
(DM 432 SO/B5200) • **Colour** White
Needle DMC Cross-Stitch No:26 (Art:1771/3)
Cross Stitch 2 strands • **Backstitch** 1 strand
French Knot 2 strands

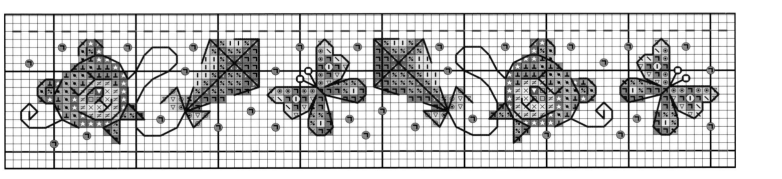

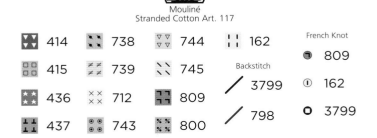

Mouliné
Stranded Cotton Art. 117

▼▼	414		738	▽▽	744	‖	162	
⊞⊞	415		739	╲╲	745			**French Knot**
★★	436	✕✕	712		809			◐ 809
⊥⊥	437	⊙⊙	743	✕✕	800			◑ 162
								O 3799

Backstitch
╱ 3799
╱ 798

Fabric DMC 28 ct Linen Fabric
(DM 432 SO/B5200) • **Colour** White
Needle DMC Cross-Stitch No:26 (Art:1771/3)
Cross Stitch 2 strands • **Backstitch** 1 strand
French Knot 2 strands

Going on Safari

What's not to love about a friendly lion, girae, cat and bird going on safari together among lots of colourful butterflies? What adventures they will have. Sew this design as a picture for the nursery wall and make up lots of stories together about this friendly bunch.

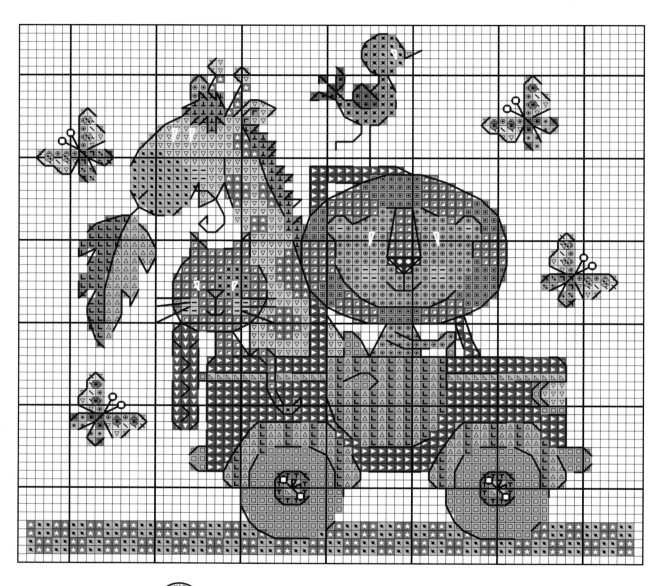

Mouliné
Stranded Cotton Art. 117

▼ 414	L L 166	738	743	209		**Backstitch**	
415	△ 165	603	▽ 744	210		╱ 310	
911	434	605	╲ 745	211		╱ 3799	
T T 913	★ 436	3853	809			**French Knot**	
955	437	3854	800			● 209	
						● 800	
						O 3799	

Fabric DMC 28 ct Linen Fabric
(DM 432 SO/B5200) • **Colour** White
Needle DMC Cross-Stitch No:26 (Art:1771/3)
Cross Stitch 2 strands • **Backstitch** 1 strand
French Knot 2 strands

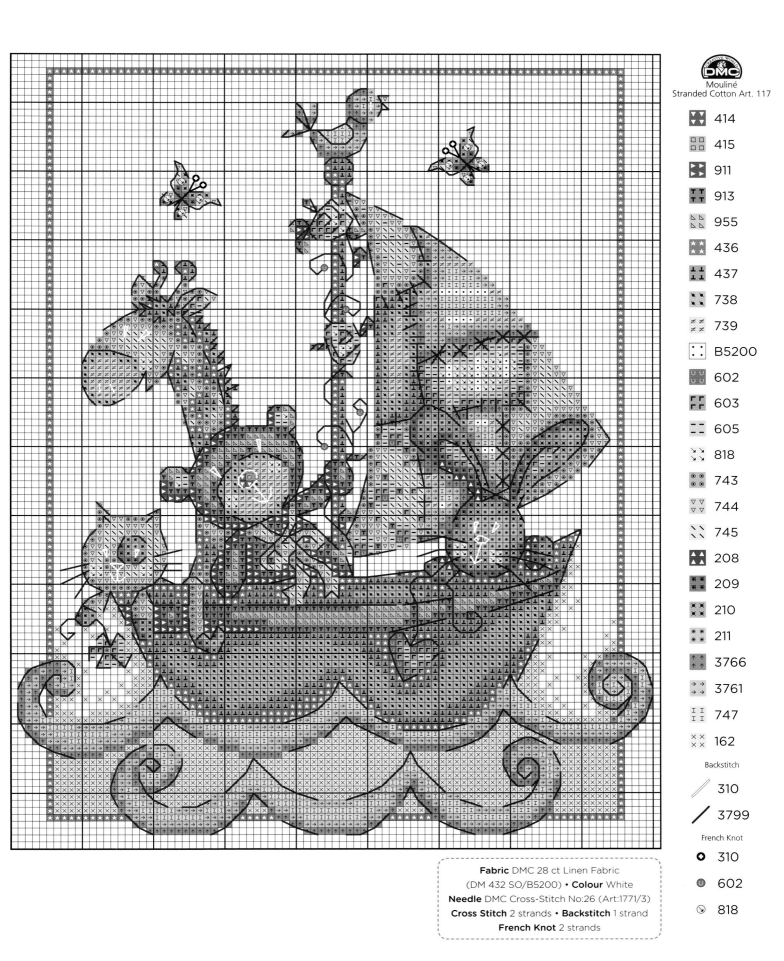

DMC
Mouliné
Stranded Cotton Art. 117

414
415
911
913
955
436
437
738
739
B5200
602
603
605
818
743
744
745
208
209
210
211
3766
3761
747
162

Backstitch

310
3799

French Knot

310
602
818

Fabric DMC 28 ct Linen Fabric
(DM 432 SO/B5200) • **Colour** White
Needle DMC Cross-Stitch No:26 (Art:1771/3)
Cross Stitch 2 strands • **Backstitch** 1 strand
French Knot 2 strands

Celebrate!

These adorable animals look like they could be deciding where to hang the bunting for a celebration. Why not stitch this for your own celebration of your new family member. It would be an ideal design to add your babies name, weight and date of birth to, to create a beautiful birth sampler for the nursery wall to celebrate and cherish this special event.

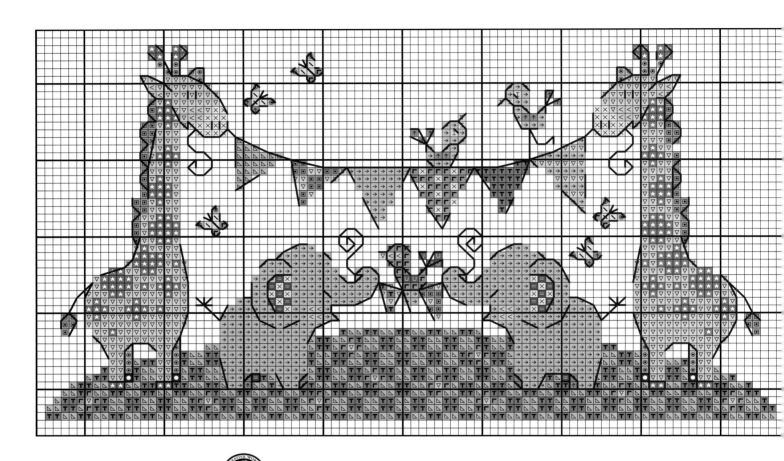

Mouliné
Stranded Cotton Art. 117

									Backstitch
T T	913	X X	712	▣ ▣	3854	▬ ▬	518	╱	3799
◿ ◿	955	< <	963	◉ ◉	743	↑ ↑	519		
◵ ◵	434	U U	602	▽ ▽	744	→ →	3761		
★ ★	436	⌐⌐	603	◸ ◸	745	I I	747		

Fabric DMC 28 ct Linen Fabric
(DM 432 SO/B5200) • **Colour** White
Needle DMC Cross-Stitch No:26 (Art:1771/3)
Cross Stitch 2 strands • **Backstitch** 1 strand

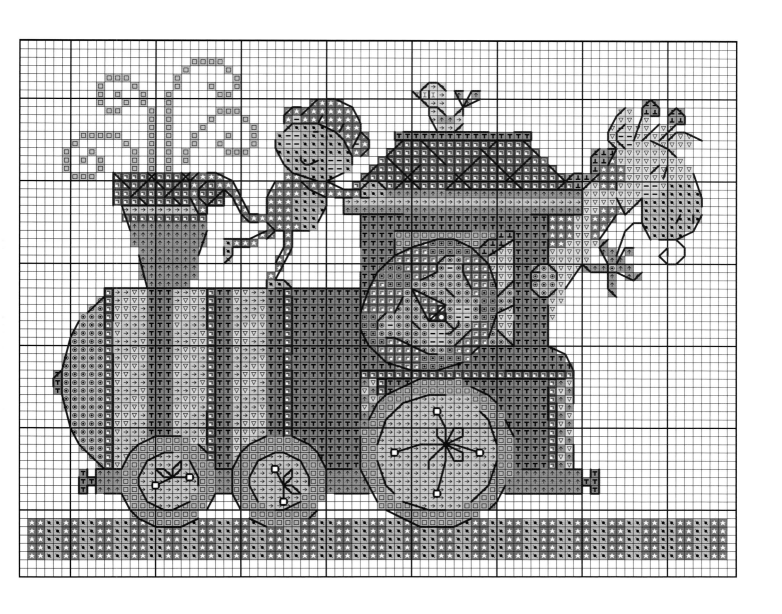

DMC
Mouliné
Stranded Cotton Art. 117

					Backstitch
▫▫ 415	⊥⊥ 437	▣▣ 3854	→→ 3761	/ 3799
⊤⊤ 913	◥◥ 738	◉◉ 743	ɪɪ 747	French Knot
▦▦ 434	⁼⁼ 605	▽▽ 744	▣▣ 350	O 3799
★★ 436	▦▦ 3853	↑↑ 519		

Fabric DMC 28 ct Linen Fabric
(DM 432 SO/B5200) • Colour White
Needle DMC Cross-Stitch No:26 (Art:1771/3)
Cross Stitch 2 strands • Backstitch 1 strand
French Knot 2 strands

Tortoise Trio

How fun and unusual is it to see three friendly tortoises carrying a flowerpot on their backs? These cute little fellows are on their way to help you celebrate the birth of your new little one, why not sew them as a picture for the nursery wall, you could even add a flower button onto the largest one's hat to add interest to the finished design.

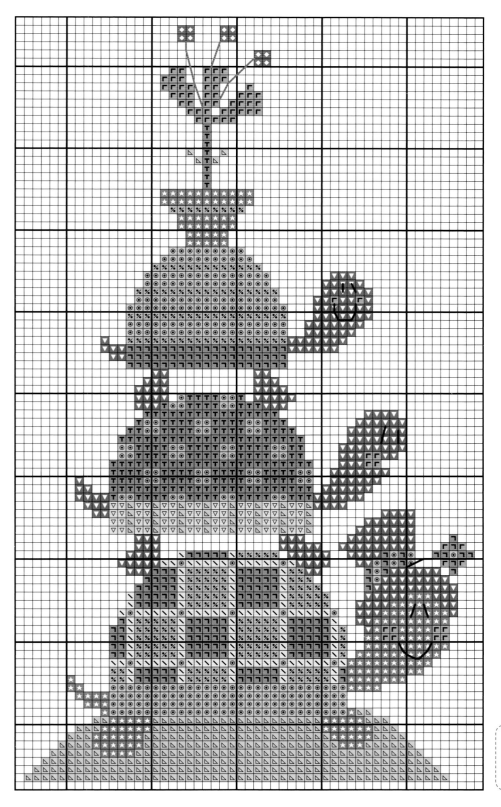

Mouliné
Stranded Cotton Art. 117

▼▼	414
TT	913
▵▵	955
★★	436
✚✚	961
ГГ	603
⊙⊙	743
▽▽	744
＼＼	745
ᒣᒣ	809
✕✕	800

Backstitch

╱	3799
╱	961

Fabric DMC 28 ct Linen Fabric
(DM 432 SO/B5200) • **Colour** White
Needle DMC Cross-Stitch No:26 (Art:1771/3)
Cross Stitch 2 strands • **Backstitch** 1 strand

Laundry Day

If laundry day looked this adorable, it might not be such a chore! This cute little design features a washing line full of freshly laundered items for the new baby, being watched over by a sweet little yellow bird. Why not stitch it and incorporate it into the nursery laundry bag?

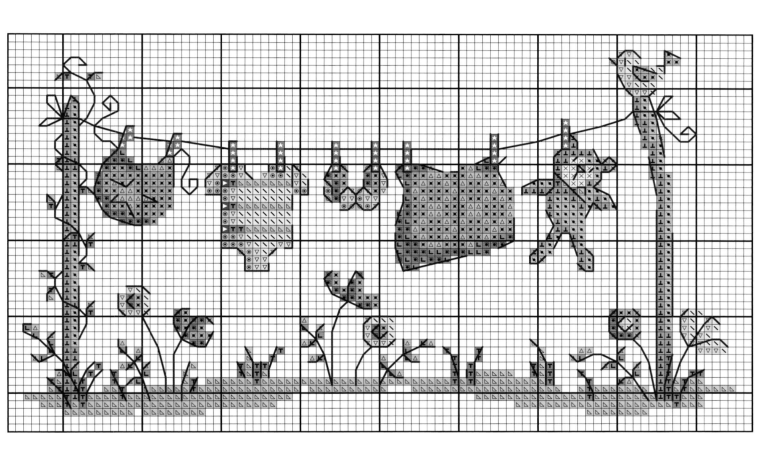

DMC
Mouliné
Stranded Cotton Art. 117

							Backstitch
911	955	165	437	712	744	209	3799
913	166	436	738	743	745	210	

Fabric DMC 28 ct Linen Fabric
(DM 432 SO/B5200) • **Colour** White
Needle DMC Cross-Stitch No:26 (Art:1771/3)
Cross Stitch 2 strands • **Backstitch** 1 strand

MONDAY

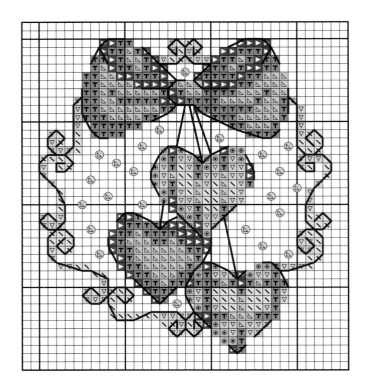

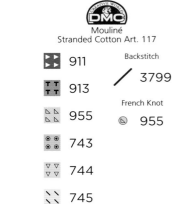

DMC
Mouliné
Stranded Cotton Art. 117

�	911	Backstitch
T T T	913	/ 3799
◣◣	955	French Knot
◉◉	743	◉ 955
▽▽	744	
◥◥	745	

Fabric DMC 28 ct Linen Fabric
(DM 432 SO/B5200) • **Colour** White
Needle DMC Cross-Stitch No:26 (Art:1771/3)
Cross Stitch 2 strands • **Backstitch** 1 strand
French Knot 2 strands

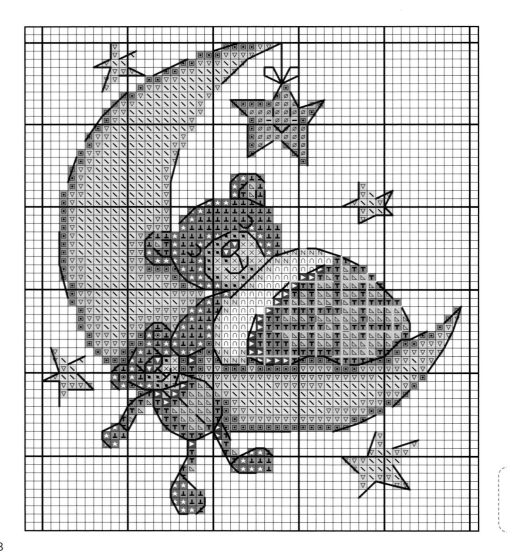

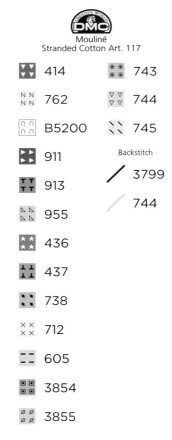

DMC
Mouliné
Stranded Cotton Art. 117

▽▽	414		◉◉	743
N N N	762		▽▽	744
∩∩	B5200		◥◥	745
►►	911			Backstitch
T T T	913		/	3799
◣◣	955		/	744
★★	436			
⊥⊥	437			
✦✦	738			
✕✕	712			
⊏⊐	605			
◉◉	3854			
∅∅	3855			

Fabric DMC 28 ct Linen Fabric
(DM 432 SO/B5200) • **Colour** White
Needle DMC Cross-Stitch No:26 (Art:1771/3)
Cross Stitch 2 strands • **Backstitch** 1 strand

Hanging Hearts & Sleepy Bears

These three designs have so many possibilities in the nursery. Why not stitch the little sleepy bear, on the moon and display him in a hoop as modern wall art? Or with the addition of your babies name, he would make an cute name plaque. And stitch the beautiful little hanging hearts with images of a baby in a pram, cot and swaddled tight in a blanket to make a lovely central panel to a cushion to adorn a chair in the nursery. Alternatively if you stitched only one of the hearts and added a real bow in place of the sewn one it would make a wonderful embellishment for a card.

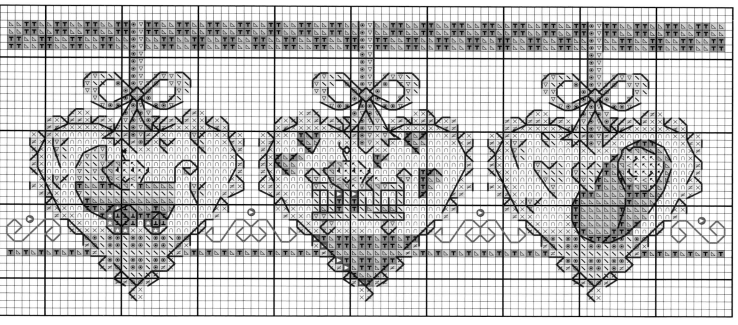

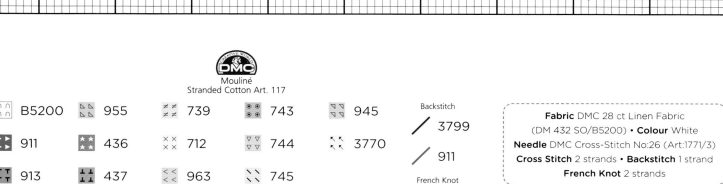

Mouliné
Stranded Cotton Art. 117

B5200	955	739	743	945	**Backstitch**
911	436	712	744	3770	3799
913	437	963	745		911

French Knot
911

Fabric DMC 28 ct Linen Fabric
(DM 432 SO/B5200) • **Colour** White
Needle DMC Cross-Stitch No:26 (Art:1771/3)
Cross Stitch 2 strands • **Backstitch** 1 strand
French Knot 2 strands

THURSDAY

WEDNESDAY FRIDAY

MONDAY

Bunny Friends

Bunnies are such cute animals, and like teddies make a lovely addition to any nursery. These designs in their subtle greens, yellows and browns are calming and tranquil and suiting both boys and girls they have a wealth of posible uses. Why not stitch either of them and patch it onto a journal cover to give as a gift. You could even pick out a small element from the designs such as the hearts, butterflies or bird to stitch seperately and make a little gift tag to accompany your gift.

Mouliné
Stranded Cotton Art. 117

414	B5200	955	738	605	745	
415	911	436	739	743	**Backstitch**	
762	913	437	712	744	3799	

Fabric DMC 28 ct Linen Fabric (DM 432 SO/B5200) • **Colour** White
Needle DMC Cross-Stitch No:26 (Art:1771/3)
Cross Stitch 2 strands • **Backstitch** 1 strand

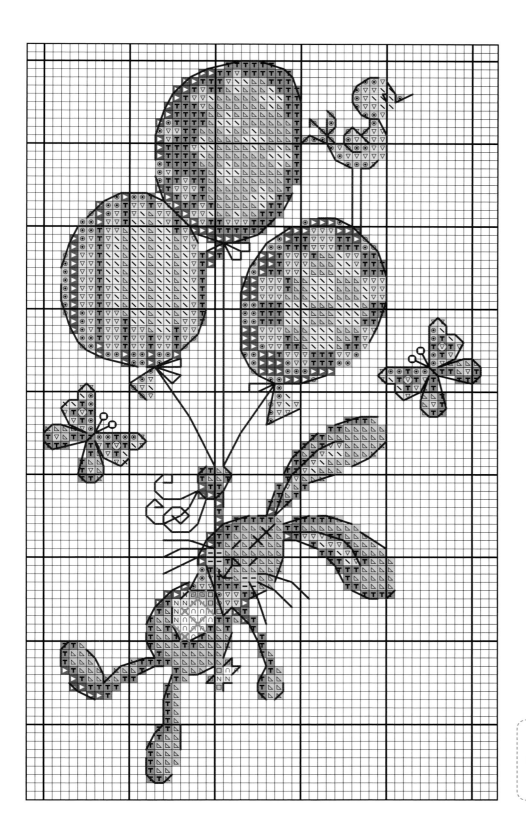

Mouliné
Stranded Cotton Art. 117

415	
762	
B5200	
911	
913	
955	
605	
743	
744	
745	

Backstitch

3799

913

French Knot

3799

744

Fabric DMC 28 ct Linen Fabric
(DM 432 SO/B5200) • **Colour** White
Needle DMC Cross-Stitch No:26 (Art:1771/3)
Cross Stitch 2 strands • **Backstitch** 1 strand
French Knot 2 strands

A New Baby Girl

What could be better to help you celebrate the arrival of your new baby girl than these designs featuring delicate pink booties, a sleeping baby, lots of roses, flowers and shades of pink? Stitch these two designs to make into journal or photograph album covers. Or to embellish gorgeous handmade cards, you could even add little real bows to the booties and cot top, and a little felt heart to enhance the handmade feel.

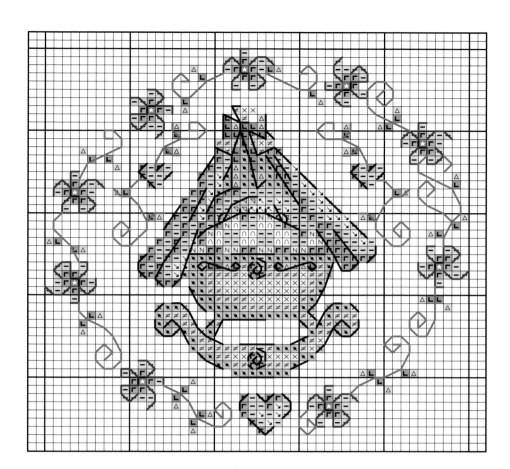

Mouliné
Stranded Cotton Art. 117

N N N	762	= =	605
∩ ∩	B5200	✕ ✕	818
L L	166	∖ ∖	945
△ △	165	✕ ✕	3770
★ ★	436		Backstitch
∴ ∴	738	/	3799
≠ ≠	739	/	581
✕ ✕	712	/	3831
Γ Γ	603		

Fabric DMC 28 ct Linen Fabric
(DM 432 SO/B5200) • **Colour** White
Needle DMC Cross-Stitch No:26 (Art:1771/3)
Cross Stitch 2 strands • **Backstitch** 1 strand

Mouliné
Stranded Cotton Art. 117

☐ ☐	415
N N N	762
∩ ∩	B5200
Γ Γ	603
= =	605
∖ ∖	818
∘ ∘	819
▽ ▽	744
∖ ∖	745
	Backstitch
/	3799
	French Knot
⊖	605

Fabric DMC 28 ct Linen Fabric
(DM 432 SO/B5200) • **Colour** White
Needle DMC Cross-Stitch No:26 (Art:1771/3)
Cross Stitch 2 strands • **Backstitch** 1 strand
French Knot 2 strands

A New Baby Boy

Celebrate the arrival of your new baby boy with these cute toyroom designs. Why not stitch the toyroom shelf onto aida and use it to decorate a toy bag or box? Or alternatively it would make a beautiful name or birth sampler. The sleeping bunny would be ideal framed and placed on the wall of the nursery, and why not add felt stars to add to the handmade feel of the picture.

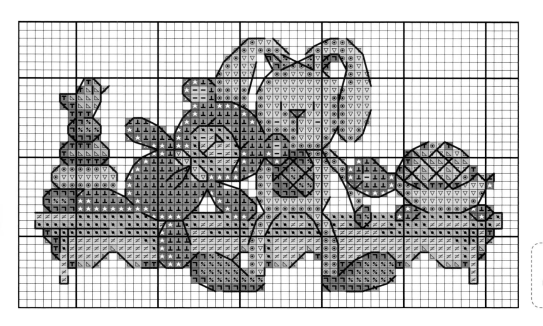

DMC
Mouliné
Stranded Cotton Art. 117

913		743
955		744
436		809
437		800
738		Backstitch
739		3799

Fabric DMC 28 ct Linen Fabric (DM 432 SO/B5200) • **Colour** White
Needle DMC Cross-Stitch No:26 (Art:1771/3)
Cross Stitch 2 strands • **Backstitch** 1 strand

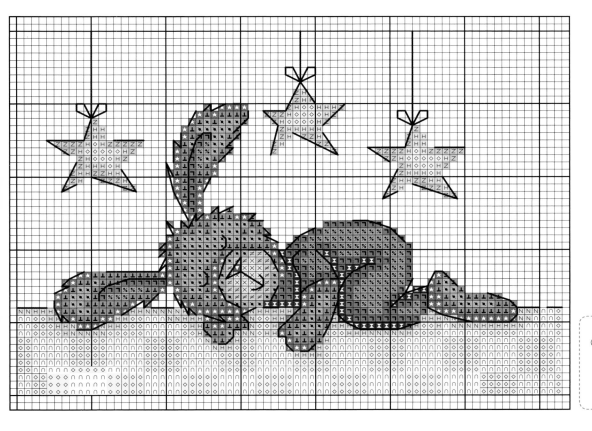

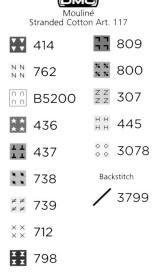

DMC
Mouliné
Stranded Cotton Art. 117

414		809
762		800
B5200		307
436		445
437		3078
738		Backstitch
739		3799
712		
798		

Fabric DMC 28 ct Linen Fabric (DM 432 SO/B5200) • **Colour** White
Needle DMC Cross-Stitch No:26 (Art:1771/3)
Cross Stitch 2 strands
Backstitch 1 strand

Sweet Little Bands

These sweet little bands with their hearts, flowers and butterflies have an array of possible uses, you could stitch them as repeat patterns onto matching aida band and use them to decorate bags, boxes, cot blankets, towels, even curtain trims and tie backs. Or alternatively you could sew elements from the designs, a heart as a gift tag, or a butterfly for a card embellishment. I'm sure you will see more and more possibilies with them once you get started stitching for baby.

Mouliné
Stranded Cotton Art. 117

913	605	3855	211	
955	818	209	**Backstitch**	
603	3854	210	/ 3799	
			/ 913	
			/ 209	

> **Fabric** DMC 28 ct Linen Fabric
> (DM 432 SO/B5200) • **Colour** White
> **Needle** DMC Cross-Stitch No:26 (Art:1771/3)
> **Cross Stitch** 2 strands • **Backstitch** 1 strand

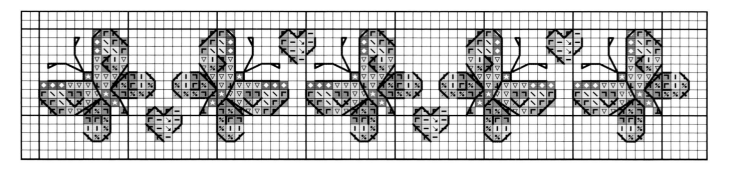

Mouliné
Stranded Cotton Art. 117

436	961	605	744	809	162
437	603	818	745	800	**Backstitch**
					/ 3799

> **Fabric** DMC 28 ct Linen Fabric
> (DM 432 SO/B5200) • **Colour** White
> **Needle** DMC Cross-Stitch No:26 (Art:1771/3)
> **Cross Stitch** 2 strands • **Backstitch** 1 strand

James
Simpson

24.8.17

7lb 6oz

Celebration Toy Sampler

Stitching a birth sampler is a lovely way to celebrate the birth of your new little one. The cute toys in this one arranged around the central, framed details make a lovely addition to any nursery and it would be treasured for generations to come. Stitch the pink version for your new little baby girl, and the blue one for a new little baby boy. But if you are not sure which to expect then the colours can be easily swapped to greens to make it a sampler suitable for all.

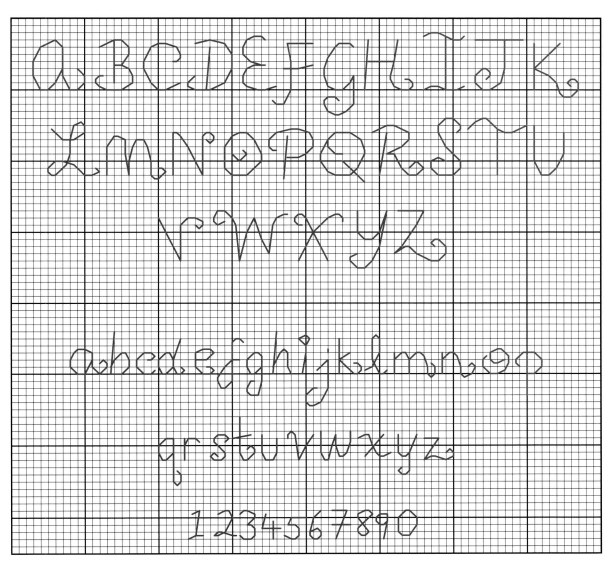

Mouliné
Stranded Cotton Art. 117

414	437	809	3855	**Backstitch**	**French Knot**
415	738	800	743	310	798
B5200	739	162	744	838	809
434	712	963	745	798	838
436	798	3854			

Fabric DMC 28 ct Linen Fabric
(DM 432 SO/B5200) • **Colour** White
Needle DMC Cross-Stitch No:26 (Art:1771/3)
Cross Stitch 2 strands • **Backstitch** 1 strand
French Knot 2 strands

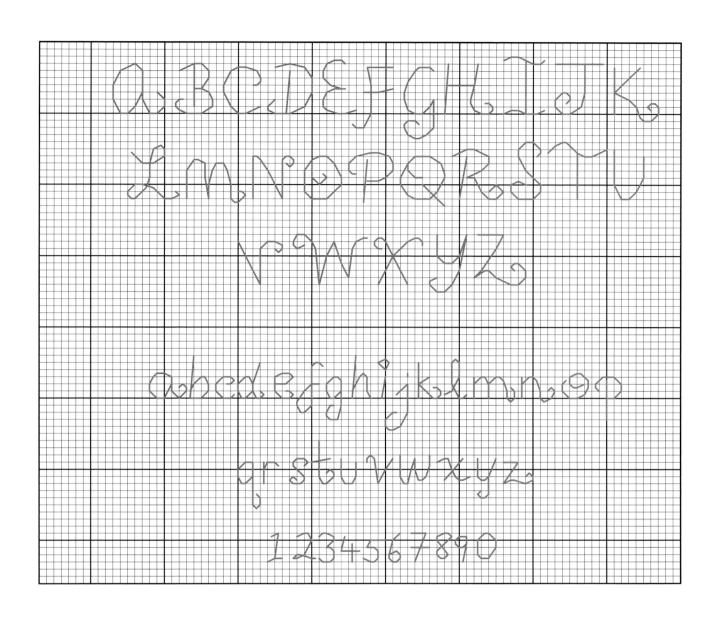

Mouliné
Stranded Cotton Art. 117

414	437	603	3855	Backstitch	French Knot
415	738	605	743	310	602
B5200	739	818	744	838	603
434	712	963	745	602	838
436	602	3854			

Fabric DMC 28 ct Linen Fabric
(DM 432 SO/B5200) • **Colour** White
Needle DMC Cross-Stitch No:26 (Art:1771/3)
Cross Stitch 2 strands • **Backstitch** 1 strand
French Knot 2 strands

The Stitches

This section shows how to work the stitches used in the book. When following these instructions, note that stitching is over one block of Aida or two threads of evenweave.

Starting and Finishing Thread

To start off your first length of thread, make a knot at one end and push the needle through to the back of the fabric, about 3cm ($1^1/4$in) from your starting point, leaving the knot on the right side. Stitch towards the knot, securing the thread at the back of the fabric as you go. When the thread is secure, cut off the knot.

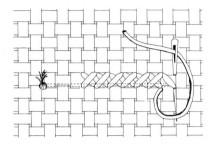

To finish off a thread or start new threads, simply weave the thread into the back of several stitches.

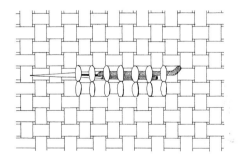

Backstitch

Backstitch is indicated on the charts by a solid coloured line. It is worked around areas of completed cross stitches to add definition, or on top of stitches to add detail.

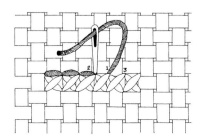

To work backstitch, pull the needle through the hole in the fabric at 1 and back through at 2. For the next stitch, pull the needle through at 3, then push to the back at 1, and repeat the process to make the next stitch. If working backstitch on an evenweave fabric, wovrk each backstitch over two threads.

Cross Stitch

Each coloured square on a chart represents one complete cross stitch. Cross stitch is worked in two easy stages. Start by working one diagonal stitch over one block of Aida or two threads of evenweave, then work a second diagonal stitch over the first stitch, but in the opposite direction to form a cross.

A cross stitch on Aida fabric.

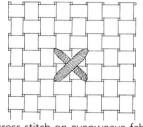

A cross stitch on evenweave fabric.

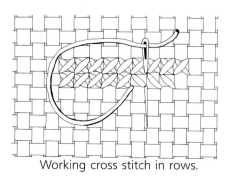

Working cross stitch in rows.

Cross stitches can be worked in rows if you have a large area to cover. Work a row of half cross stitches in one direction and then back in the opposite direction with the diagonal stitches to complete each cross. The upper stitches of all the crosses should lie in the same direction to produce a neat effect.

Half Cross Stitch

This stitch is also used if you chose to work a design on canvas in tapestry wool (yarn), replacing whole cross stitches with half stitches. A half cross stitch is simply one half of a cross stitch, with the diagonal facing the same way as the upper stitches of each complete cross stitch.

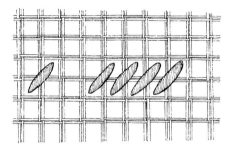

French Knots

These are small knots used for details, indicated on charts by coloured dots.

To work a French knot, bring the needle through to the front of the fabric, just above the point you want the stitch placed. Wind the thread once around the needle and, holding the twisted thread firmly, insert the needle a little away from its starting position. Two tips for working French knots: never rush them and never go back into the same point where your thread came up or your knot will pull through to the back.

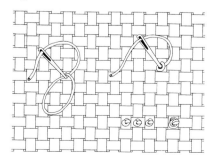